Changes

A Child's First Poetry Collection

Changes

A Child's First Poetry Collection

Charlotte Zolotow
Tiphanie Beeke

Introduction by Crescent Dragonwagon

sourcebooks
jabberwocky

Copyright © 2015 by Charlotte Zolotow
Cover and internal design © 2015 by Sourcebooks, Inc.
Cover design by Sourcebooks, Inc.
Illustrations © Tiphanie Beeke

Sourcebooks and the colophon are registered trademarks of Sourcebooks, Inc.

The digitally-created illustrations incorporate colored pencil sketches and mixed media.

Published by Sourcebooks Jabberwocky, an imprint of Sourcebooks, Inc.
P.O. Box 4410, Naperville, Illinois 60567-4410
(630) 961-3900
Fax: (630) 961-2168
www.jabberwockykids.com

Originally published in 1967 in the United States of America by Harper & Row, Publishers; 1970 in the United States of America by Thomas Y. Crowell; 1987 in the United States of America by Harcourt Brace Jovanovich, Publishers.

Library of Congress Cataloging-in-Publication data is on file with the publisher.

Source of Production: Leo Paper, Heshan City, Guangdong Province, China
Date of Production: January 2015
Run Number: 5002890

Printed and bound in China.

LEO 10 9 8 7 6 5 4 3 2 1

The Poems

Celebrating the Seasons

Summer

Autumn

Winter

A Celebration of Charlotte Zolotow

I'm overjoyed to introduce *Changes: A Child's First Poetry Collection*, which includes a selection of twenty-eight poems written by Charlotte Zolotow, my mother.

Charlotte was the author of more than ninety published books for children. Some won awards—among them, two Caldecott Honors. Others were called "groundbreaking"—*William's Doll, My Grandson Lew.* But, simultaneously, she was an editor-publisher at Harper & Row (Harper Brothers in the early years of her tenure there; HarperCollins by the time she left). She worked with many of the great children's book and YA authors of the '50s, '60s, '70s, and '80s, including Laura Ingalls Wilder, Maurice Sendak, Paul Zindel, Francesca Lia Block, and Arnold Lobel.

She was married to Maurice Zolotow, a show business biographer, and had two children. Her son, Stephen (Zee), plays poker for a living. And I am her daughter, born Ellen, renamed Crescent Dragonwagon in 1969, also a writer.

Charlotte died at age ninety-eight, in 2013, in the home she had lived in for more than fifty-five years.

These poems of hers are deceptively simple, transparent, and refreshing as a glass of clean, clear, cold spring-water. They follow the turning circle of a year's seasons, and I think they will introduce not only the pleasures and surprises of the seasons, but also those of poetry itself, to young readers.

That they are being published in 2015—which would have been the year of Charlotte's 100th birthday—adds to my pleasure, and, I hope, to that of this book's readers, as well as their parents and teachers...child-loving adults who, most likely, grew up on Charlotte's books themselves.

This, too, like the seasons, and the year of this publication being her centenary year, makes a kind of circle.

These poems reflect, as Charlotte herself did, on what stays the same and what changes; on how every moment, each flower, the breeze, and the sky, is ever-altering and unique (and should be celebrated in its one-of-a-kindness). And yet, in the face of all this change—and here is Charlotte's reassuring genius, her ability to frame the largest, boldest truths for the smallest, newest readers—there is a comforting cyclical repetition.

Because of Charlotte's words, spoken and in her books, and because of her poems, our vision is changed and sharpened. When we and her young readers see the wonders of this bittersweet, lovely, transient world, we watch with eyes that are now, partly, hers. Although she is gone, she is, thus, still here: part of the cycle she celebrated.

—Crescent Dragonwagon, Saxtons River, Vermont, Fall 2014

Celebrating the Seasons

Change

This summer
still hangs
heavy and sweet
with sunlight
as it did last year.

The autumn
still comes
showering cold and crimson
as it did last year.

The winter
still stings
clean and cold and white
as it did last year.

The spring
still comes
like a whisper in the dark night.

It is only I
who have changed.

Spring

River Winding

Rain falling, what things do you grow?
Snow melting, where do you go?
Wind blowing, what trees do you know?
River winding, where do you flow?

The Spring Wind

The summer wind
is soft and sweet
the winter wind is strong
the autumn wind is mischievous
and sweeps the leaves along.

The wind I love the best
comes gently after rain
smelling of spring and growing things
brushing the world with feathery wings
while everything glistens, and everything sings
in the spring wind
after the rain.

Lying in the Grass

Lying in the grass
looking up through the trees
at the sky,
I saw a small bird
flying over the trees
high high high.

He dipped and he swooped
and flew to rest
on the branch of the tree
far above me.

And watching him
as I lay there,
        I wondered
if he could see
lying in the grass
looking at the sky,
something odd to him
which was
            me!

16

Violets

Someone is coming
down the road
and they may buy
a bunch of our violets
purple and sweet
smelling of spring.
But we won't tell
the secret place
where they grow.
No one will know
the tall grass
where we found them.
No one can buy
the feeling of the hot sun
on our hair
as we picked them.
It is only the flowers themselves
the violets
purple and sweet
they'll take away.

Crocus

Little crocus
like a cup,
holding all that sunlight up!

Pansies

Pansies purple
pansies blue
their funny faces
remind me of you.

For whether they're yellow
or reddish or blue,
they seem to be smiling
just like you.

Summer

You

I like shadows
I like sun
I like you
more than anyone.

I like summer
I like the cold
I'll even like you
when you're old.

I like work
I like play
I like you
     every which way.

A Moment in Summer

A moment in summer
belongs to me
and one particular
honey bee.
A moment in summer
shimmering clear
making the sky
seem very near,
a moment in summer
belongs to me.

Blue

Blue is a good color.
                    Blue
as the sea at noon.
                    Blue
as bluejays
and blueberries
and soft sweet plums.

Blue
as bachelor buttons
and larkspur
and a new baby's eyes.
            Blue
as the sky itself.

By the Sea

The salty wind
the sound of the sea,
the sand and the sun,
the waves and the spray—
a glistening, glittering
                    jewel of a day!

The Bridge

Glittering bridge,
curved like a harp
with your necklace of sparkling lights,
how you shine through the dark
of these silent summer nights!

The Fly

I was sitting on the porch
reading my book
in the summer sun.

A fly
settled on my page
black as ink.

Quivering and alive,
rubbing one leg against the other,
he sat on a word.

Beetle

Shining Japanese beetle
eating the rose,
how your wings
glisten
like a small rainbow
in the sun!

Autumn

A Dog

I am alone.
Someone is raking leaves
outside

and there is one yellow leaf
on the black branch
brushing the window.

Suddenly a wet nose
nuzzles
my empty hand.

Autumn

Now the summer is grown old,
the light long summer
                    is grown old.

Leaves change
and the garden is gold
with marigolds and zinnias
tangled and bold,
blazing blazing
orange and gold.

            The light long summer
            is grown old.

School Day

I don't mean to look
but I can't help seeing
a bit of sky outside the schoolhouse window.

I don't mean to watch
but I can't help watching
the maple branch that brushes against the pane.

I don't mean to dream
but I can't help dreaming
that I could be wandering
under the sky,

        watching the leaves
        watching the trees
        as the wind goes by.

The Leaves

The world is weeping leaves today
golden, crimson, brown,
drifting slowly down.

Lovely autumn, please do stay
here in this little town!

The world is weeping leaves today,
golden, crimson, brown.

Halloween

The moon is full and
the night is strange,
filled with mystery.

From the shadows
under the tree
three small white ghosts
are coming up the walk
to me.

Look

Firelight and shadows
dancing on the wall.
Look at my shadow
    TEN FEET TALL!

Winter

The First Snow

There is a special kind of quiet
that each of us knows.
We hear it in our sleep
the first night it snows.

The silence stirs behind our dreams.
Something lovely calls.
Softly we wake to whiteness
as the first snow falls.

River in Winter

The ice moves slowly
        down the river
the gulls
    are circling
        high
grey and white
grey and white
against
   the
     grey-blue
        sky!

Scene

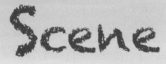

Little trees like pencil strokes
black and still
etched forever in my mind
on that snowy hill.

Contrast

As I watch the snow fall,
big, slow white flakes
like feathers floating down,
my hands are cold.

It's hard to remember
the summer
and soaking up the sun,
feeling its warmth
seep through me
deep through me
down to these frozen toes.

North and South

Christmas again,
holly and pine,
bells and berries,
things that shine.

Christmas again,
but far away
palm trees drip
with ocean spray!
Far away it's very sunny
but here it's cold and white...
　　　　　　　it's funny.

Here

In this spot
covered now by snow,
tangled branch and twig,
in this spot where the ice edges
and the ground is frozen
and the birds peck at bread,
in this spot
there will be
crocuses blooming
yellow and white,
holding petaled cups
of sun,
if only
spring would
come.

Sleepless Nights

One night
when I was very little,
I couldn't sleep.

My mother came
and carried me downstairs
and stood with me
looking out of our window.

The street light was on outside,
and snow was whirling, swirling,
a dazzling white
around and around the street light.
And the ground
and trees
and bushes
were icy crystal white.

I remember that night,
with the snow
white, white, white,
and my mother's arms around me
warm and tight.

So Will I

My grandfather remembers long ago
the white Queen Anne's lace that grew wild.
He remembers the buttercups and goldenrod
from when he was a child.

He remembers long ago
the white snow falling falling.
He remembers the bluebird and thrush
at twilight
calling, calling.

He remembers long ago
the new moon in the summer sky
He remembers the wind in the trees
and its long, rising sigh.
And so will I
          so will I.